Greenland

North
America

Atlantic
Ocean

N

South
America

To England
To England

CONTENTS

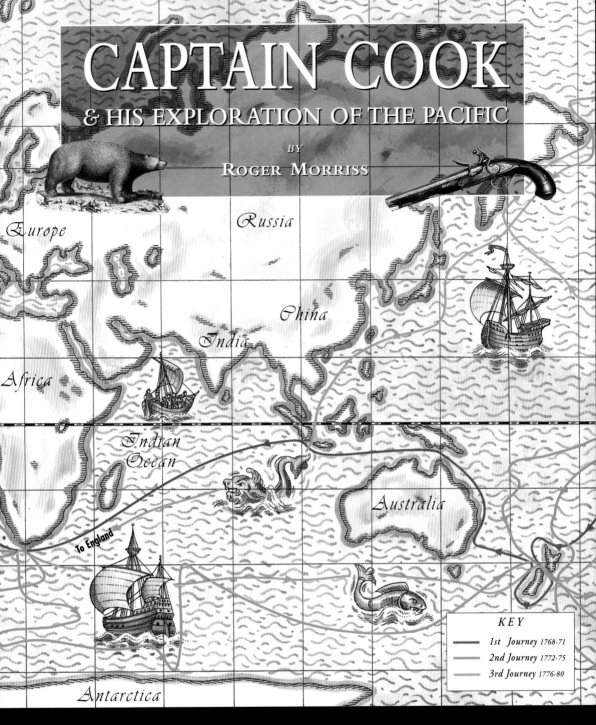

CAPTAIN COOK
& HIS EXPLORATION OF THE PACIFIC

BY
ROGER MORRISS

Europe

Russia

China

India

Africa

Indian
Ocean

Australia

To England

Antarctica

KEY

━━━ *1st Journey 1768-71*

━━━ *2nd Journey 1772-75*

━━━ *3rd Journey 1776-80*

A chart of Captain Cook's three great voyages.

Published by *ticktock* Publishing Ltd in association
with the National Maritime Museum,
Greenwich, UK and HM Bark Endeavour
Foundation, Fremantle, Australia.

snapping-turtle
guide

The World before Cook

When Cook was born in 1728, Europeans had only a sketchy knowledge of the Americas, Africa, India and the Far East. New Zealand and most of the Pacific were unknown, and all of Australia except the west coast. Europeans had long dreamt of finding a North-West Passage to the East round northern Canada. It was also believed that an inhabitable Great Southern Continent might lie where we now know there is only the frozen waste of Antarctica. Exploration was limited, partly by the hardships, malnutrition and scurvy of long sailing voyages, and by the simple methods of navigation. Thus, few British seamen had crossed the Pacific since Sir Francis Drake was the first Englishman to do so in 1577-80.

TERRESTIAL GLOBE, ABOUT 1740

Made when Cook was about 12 years old, this shows the world before the explorations of the 1760s. Although the shapes of India and south-east Asia are clearly marked, the east coast of Australia is missing, along with most of New Zealand and Van Diemen's Land, as Tasmania was known.

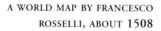

A WORLD MAP BY FRANCESCO ROSSELLI, ABOUT 1508

Printed about 15 years after Christopher Columbus returned from discovering the 'New World', Rosselli's map suggests the Americas but no Pacific Ocean. A Great Southern Continent was then thought to exist to balance the weight of the northern lands.

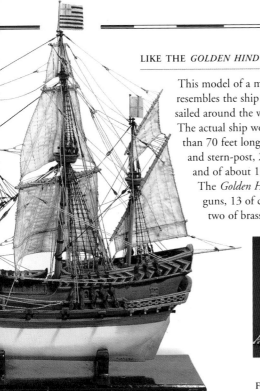

LIKE THE *GOLDEN HIND*

This model of a merchant ship resembles the ship in which Drake sailed around the world in 1577-80. The actual ship would have been less than 70 feet long between stem and stern-post, 20 feet broad, and of about 100 tons burden. The *Golden Hind* carried 15 guns, 13 of cast iron and two of brass.

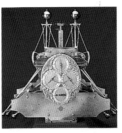

JOHN HARRISON'S FIRST CHRONOMETER

A large prize was offered to anyone who could solve the problem of finding longitude at sea. Harrison, a Yorkshire carpenter and clockmaker, did so by developing an accurate sea-clock to calculate longitude from time. This is his first experimental model, completed in 1735.

~1492~
Christopher Columbus discovers central America.

~1577~
Sir Francis Drake starts his voyage around the world.

~1588~
The Spanish Armada threatens Britain with invasion.

~1714~
Board of Longitude established to promote solutions for finding longitude (east/west position) at sea.

~1728~
Cook born at Marton-in-Cleveland, north Yorkshire.

~1729~
John Harrison starts building his first experimental chronometer.

MARINER'S ASTROLABE

Seamen used astrolabes between about 1470 and 1700 to determine their latitude by measuring the height above the horizon of the Sun at noon, or the Pole Star at night. This astrolabe was found in 1845 on the island of Valentia, Ireland, and is presumed to come from the wreck of a ship from the Spanish Armada, in 1588.

SIR FRANCIS DRAKE

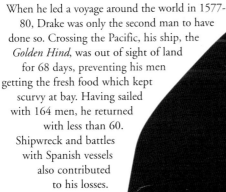

When he led a voyage around the world in 1577-80, Drake was only the second man to have done so. Crossing the Pacific, his ship, the *Golden Hind*, was out of sight of land for 68 days, preventing his men getting the fresh food which kept scurvy at bay. Having sailed with 164 men, he returned with less than 60. Shipwreck and battles with Spanish vessels also contributed to his losses.

Rivalry for Empire

When Cook was born the parts of the world conquered by European powers were still thought to belong to them. Empires provided precious metals like gold and silver, as well as timber and animal skins that could be use in trade. Spain thought the Pacific Ocean was part of her empire, which spread from the Philippine Islands in the west to central and southern America in the east. However, during wars against France and Spain, the British navy began to penetrate the Pacific, undermining the idea that it was a 'Spanish lake'. In 1740-44, Commodore George Anson attacked Spanish shipping off California before returning home via China. British forces also started attacking Spanish bases, like Porto Bello, on the mainland of central America.

COMMODORE GEORGE ANSON

In 1739 Britain and Spain began the War of Jenkins' Ear (so-called because a British merchant ship captain claimed a Spanish officer cut off his ear) and Anson took a squadron of five British naval vessels into the Pacific to attack Spanish shipping and settlements. He returned home around the world with plunder worth £400,000 but lost 1,051 of his 1,955 men, mainly from scurvy and disease.

A COMMEMORATIVE PLATE

Admiral Vernon's capture of the Spanish town of Porto Bello was celebrated in England and many commemorative items produced for sale. This plate, made in Lambeth or Liverpool in 1740, depicts the Iron Castle under bombardment, with the town beyond.

CAPTAIN COOK
-A TIME LINE-

~1739~
The War of Jenkins' Ear sees Britain invade Spanish colonial waters.

Admiral Vernon captures Spanish Porto Bello in central America.

~1740~
Anson sets sail to attack the Spanish in the Pacific, returning by way of China.

~1743~
Anson takes the Spanish treasure ship, Nuestra Señora de Covadonga.

~1744~
Anson returns home with treasure worth over £400,000.

MODEL OF A CHINESE GARDEN

After crossing the Pacific, Anson put into the Canton River, China, 1744, to refit his ship. His attitude was too aggressive for the Chinese and his presence disturbed merchants trying to maintain trade. However, he was given this model Chinese garden, the contents of which signify long life and include a peach tree in coral, a pine tree in carved wood and ivory, bamboos in tinted ivory, and rocks in malachite and rose quartz.

THE TAKING OF THE *NUESTRA SEÑORA DE COVADONGA*

While in the Pacific, Anson captured one of the Spanish treasure ships sailing from Acapulco to Manila with 1,313,843 pieces of eight and 35,682 oz. of silver on board. Worth at least £400,000 then, it would be many millions today.

THE CAPTURE OF PORTO BELLO

In 1739 a British squadron under Admiral Vernon took the Spanish coastal town of Porto Bello in central America. The town was defended by three castles, the first of which, the Iron Castle, was bombarded into submission.

SWORD SURRENDERED AT PORTO BELLO

This sword, with its Parisian hilt and Spanish blade, was surrendered by the Spanish commandant of the Iron Castle in 1739.

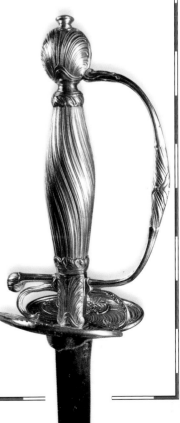

Cook's origins & early life

Shipping coal was a hard, physical trade. Ships were loaded and unloaded by manpower. Coal had to be handled in baskets and is shown here being 'whipped', or tipped down a chute. Cook managed these men and such work in the River Tyne and River Thames.

JAMES COOK, AGED 48

Cook became a naval captain and explorer of world fame. But his navigational ability was based on seafaring skills learned as a youth in the coal trade in the North Sea.

James Cook was born in a two-roomed cottage at Marton-in-Cleveland, north Yorkshire, on 7 October 1728. His father was a Scots labourer, his mother a Yorkshire woman, and they had seven children of whom four died before they passed the age of five. James at first helped his father on a farm at Great Ayton, before being apprenticed to a grocer and haberdasher at Staithes. Not liking shop-work, he was apprenticed in 1746 to John Walker, a Whitby ship-owner and captain in the coal trade, and spent the next nine years sailing from the River Tyne to London and the Baltic. Walker wanted to make him master of a ship but instead, in 1755, he volunteered for the Royal Navy.

THE CUSTOMS HOUSE, LONDON

Cook would have known the London Customs House well. Although only cargo shipped from abroad was subject to import duty, coal from the north-east of England, carried down the east coast still had to be declared.

CAPTAIN COOK
–A TIME LINE–

-1745-
Cook works for a grocer and haberdasher in Staithes.

-1746-
Cook apprenticed to a Whitby ship-owner and coal-trader.

-1755-
Cook volunteers for the Royal Navy.

THE PORT OF WHITBY

Whitby, where Cook went to sea, is on the north-east coast of England, where coal-mining close to the coast and River Tyne then made its shipment to London an important trade. Colliers were beached for loading and refitting.

A NORTH SEA COLLIER

This model of a 'cat-built bark' shows the type of ship in the coal trade. A strong, roomy hull permitted it to rest on a beach or river bed and carry much cargo.

Master's Mate

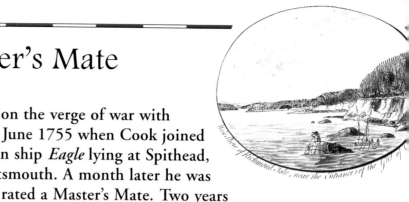

Britain was on the verge of war with France in June 1755 when Cook joined the 60-gun ship *Eagle* lying at Spithead, off Portsmouth. A month later he was rated a Master's Mate. Two years later he become a ship's master himself, sailing in the 64-gun *Pembroke* to assist the British drive the French out of Canada.

During the winter of 1758-59 Cook helped to perfect a chart of the St. Lawrence River, which permitted an expedition under General James Wolfe to seize Quebec. At the mouth of the river, the waters around the island of Newfoundland were valuable for their cod and after the war, each summer until 1767, Cook was employed making charts of the island.

A SEAMAN HEAVING THE LEAD

As the Master of a warship, Cook would often have relied on seamen sounding the depth of water beneath the ship's keel by casting a lead weight on a line over the side.

CHART OF NEWFOUNDLAND

This was one of the highly accurate charts made by James Cook and Michael Lane between 1763 and 1767. Cook did the surveying for these charts each summer, returning to London each winter to prepare the finished products for publication. Cook had married Elizabeth Betts in 1762 and lived in east London.

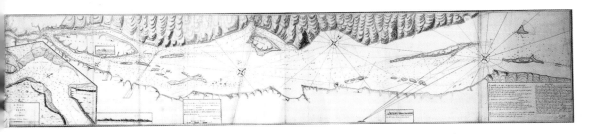

COOK'S CHART OF THE ST LAWRENCE RIVER

The chart he prepared in 1758-59 shows the numerous islands and shoals around which the army transports and naval escorts had to navigate in order to reach Quebec. Cook's chart opened the way for defeat of the French on the Heights of Abraham, which led to British possession of Canada.

CAPTAIN COOK
-A TIME LINE-

~1756~
The Seven Years War starts between Britain and France.

~1757~
Cook becomes a Master in the Royal Navy.

~1758~
Cook perfects a chart of the St Lawrence River.

~1759~
General Wolfe takes Quebec, Canada.

~1762~
Cook marries Elizabeth Betts and lives in East London.

~1763~
Cook begins charting the coastline of Newfoundland.

THE DEATH OF WOLFE AT QUEBEC

General Wolfe was shot in the battle for Quebec on 13 September 1759 and died after hearing of his victory. He was only 32 years old. His body is buried at Greenwich, London, where he lived, and where his statue now stands in the Park.

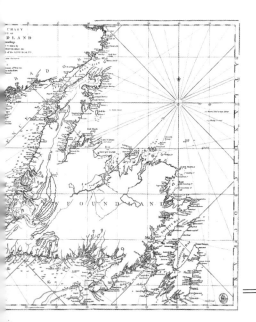

THEODOLITE 1737

When Cook charted Newfoundland, he worked in conjunction with surveyors led by Joseph Desbarres making maps on shore. Surveying instruments were already sophisticated. Theodolites, for measuring angles, had telescopic sights and rackwork circles for both the vertical and horizontal movements.

A Pacific voyage

~1760~
George III becomes King.

~1764~
*Captain Palliser appointed
Governor of Newfoundland.*

~1768~
*Cook is chosen to command
the ship to carry observers
of the Transit of Venus.*

~1770~
*Lord Sandwich becomes First
Lord of the Admiralty.*

*Captain Palliser becomes
Comptroller of the Navy
Board, under the Admiralty.*

ook was lucky in that his skill at navigation, surveying and chart-making was noticed by Sir Hugh Palliser, another Yorkshireman, who was twice Cook's captain and subsequently Governor of Newfoundland, Comptroller of the Navy, and a member of the Board of Admiralty directed by Lord Sandwich. The latter presented Cook to George III, who was much interested in scientific discoveries. Indeed, in 1768, when the Royal Society wanted to measure the distance of the Earth from the Sun by observing the 'Transit of Venus' from somewhere in the southern Pacific, he helped to finance the voyage. Cook was chosen to captain the ship sent to carry the scientists, who were led by Joseph Banks, later President of the Royal Society for forty years.

BANKS'S COLLECTIONS

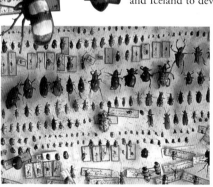

As well as sailing with Cook to New Zealand and Australia, Banks travelled to Newfoundland and Iceland to develop this collection of natural history specimens. The collection became a foundation of that now in the Natural History Museum.

JOSEPH BANKS

A wealthy young gentleman, Banks joined Cook's first voyage of exploration in the Pacific to pursue his natural history interests. He was President of the Royal Society from 1778 until 1820 and helped to publish the journals of Cook's last voyage.

[handwritten letter, Cook to Lord Sandwich, partially legible]

LORD SANDWICH

Although better known for his indulgence in London life - his name was given to food he reputedly ordered to avoid leaving the gambling table - Sandwich was an accomplished administrator and First Lord of the Admiralty from 1770 until 1782. In this role he promoted Cook after his second voyage and encouraged him to volunteer for the third. As Cook's letter to him in 1776 suggests, they became good friends and, after Cook's death, Sandwich presided over the publication of his journals.

ASTRONOMER AT HIS TRANSIT INSTRUMENT

The Astronomer Royal predicted the Transit of Venus across the face of the sun in 1769 from repeated observations at the Royal Observatory, founded in 1675 in Greenwich Park. From there, nightly observations mapped the visible universe.

GEORGE III

George III became King in 1760, at the height of the Seven Years War with France. He had a political, as well as a scientific, interest in encouraging exploration, for France was intent on enlarging her empire. Significantly, though Cook's last voyage was overshadowed by the rebellion of George III's American colonies, his journals for the voyage were published on the King's forty-eighth birthday.

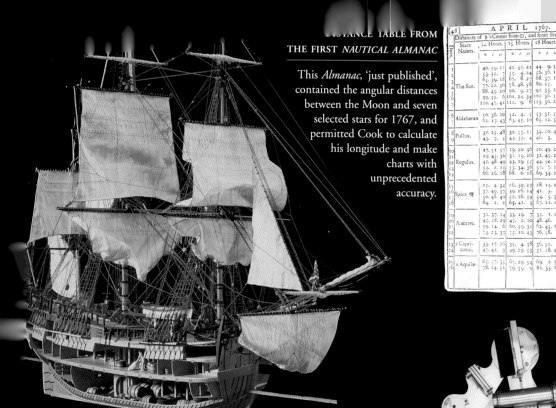

DISTANCE TABLE FROM THE FIRST *NAUTICAL ALMANAC*

This *Almanac*, 'just published', contained the angular distances between the Moon and seven selected stars for 1767, and permitted Cook to calculate his longitude and make charts with unprecedented accuracy.

[48]	APRIL 1767.			
Days	Distances of ☽'s Center from ☉, and from Stars west of			
	Stars Names.	12 Hours.	15 Hours.	18 Hours.	21 Hours
		° ′ ″	° ′ ″	° ′ ″	° ′ ″
1		40. 59. 11	42. 34. 44	44. 9. 51	45. 44.
2		53. 32. 7	55. 4. 24	56. 36. 16	58. 7.
3		65. 39. 18	67. 8. 27	68. 37. 14	70. 5.
4	The Sun.	77. 22. 36	78. 48. 58	80. 15. 1	81. 40.
5		88. 45. 20	90. 9. 27	91. 33. 11	92. 57.
6		99. 52. 6	101. 14. 34	102. 36. 52	103. 59.
7		110. 47. 42	112. 9. 6	113. 30. 25	114. 51.
6	Aldebaran	50. 36. 10	52. 4. 5	53. 31. 57	54. 59.
7		62. 17. 43	63. 45. 10	65. 12. 34	66. 39.
8	Pollux.	31. 25. 48	32. 53. 11	34. 20. 40	35. 48.
9		43. 7. 5	44. 35. 4	46. 3. 8	47. 31.
10		17. 51. 57	19. 20. 36	20. 49. 26	22. 18.
11		29. 45. 36	31. 15. 20	32. 45. 26	34. 15
12	Regulus.	41. 48. 40	43. 19. 55	44. 51. 10	46. 22
13		54. 2. 11	55. 34. 38	57. 7. 11	58. 39
14		66. 26. 18	68. 0. 18	69. 34. 20	71. 8
15		25. 4. 34	26. 39. 23	28. 14. 26	29. 49.
16	Spica ♍	37. 49. 37	39. 26. 14	41. 3. 5	42. 40.
17		50. 48. 40	52. 26. 59	54. 5. 31	55. 44.
18		64. 1. 2	65. 41. 3	67. 21. 18	69. 1.
19		31. 37. 14	33. 19. 7	35. 1. 13	36. 43.
20	Antares.	45. 18. 29	47. 2. 10	48. 46. 5	50. 30.
21		59. 14. 6	60. 59. 31	62. 45. 11	64. 31.
22		73. 25. 37	75. 10. 43	76. 56. 2	78. 45.
23	α Capri-	33. 17. 26	35. 4. 38	36. 52. 4	38. 39.
24	corni.	47. 41. 9	49. 29. 53	51. 18. 44	53. 7.
25	α Aquilæ.	65. 57. 35	67. 29. 54	69. 2. 36	70. 35.
26		78. 24. 51	79. 59. 9	81. 33. 29	83. 7.

A MODEL OF THE *ENDEAVOUR*

This model demonstrates what the *Endeavour* looked like when she was purchased in 1768. Previously named the *Earl of Pembroke*, she was of 369 tons and cost £2,800. She was armed with six carriage guns and eight swivel guns. With her large storage capacity, she carried twelve months' supply of all provisions except beer, of which there was enough for one month. Most supplies were stored in the hold and, when fully laden, her draught was 14 feet.

DOLLOND TELESCOPE

Cook applied to the Admiralty for a supply of navigational, chart-making and astronomical instruments. Advances in the design of these instruments gave Cook the ability to navigate accurately and record his discoveries for posterity exactly. His navigational instruments included a telescope like this one made by Peter Dollond of London, who made the best available at the time. Since the 1750s telescopes had been made with an achromatic object glass that reduced the size of the telescope and rendered objects practically free of colour distortion.

Preparations

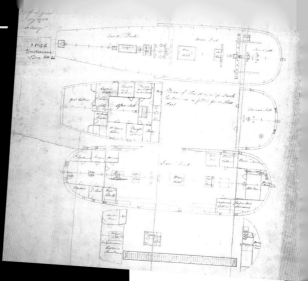

In April 1768 the Admiralty purchased the *Endeavour*, a three-year-old Whitby collier like those Cook had already sailed in the North Sea. She was only 106 feet long on her upper deck, but her hull was strong enough to rest on shore to receive repairs, and capacious enough, with squeezing, to carry 94 people, victuals, stores and equipment. While she was refitted in Deptford Dockyard, Cook obtained navigational equipment, now including the first *Nautical Almanac*, published by the Astronomer Royal in 1766. Meanwhile the Royal Society appointed naturalists to collect plants, artists to record what they saw, and an astronomer to observe the Transit of Venus.

DECK PLANS OF THE *ENDEAVOUR*

As generally in the navy, the ships' officers and senior civilians exercised on the quarterdeck. To accommodate the extra passengers, the decks of the *Endeavour* were subdivided into more cabins. The crew and civilian servants slept in hammocks slung above stores on the lower deck. The hold, containing further provisions, was reached through hatches covered by gratings.

COOK'S SEXTANT

Oceanic navigation demanded an instrument that accurately measured the altitude of heavenly bodies. The backstaff, invented by John Davis in 1590, was still in use, but had been improved upon by John Hadley in 1734 with his quadrant or octant, and by the sextant in 1757. Cook took this sextant, made by Jesse Ramsden of London about 1770, on his third voyage.

LAUNCHING A SHIP AT DEPTFORD DOCKYARD

When the *Endeavour* was docked at Deptford, her hull was given an extra skin of wooden sheathing, her masts and yards were replaced, and partitions for extra cabins were inserted. After being refloated, she was rigged and equipped from the great storehouse. Food supplies were obtained from the Deptford victualling yard.

CAPTAIN COOK
-A Time Line-

~1766~
The first *Nautical Almanac* published by the Astronomer Royal.

~1768~
A Whitby collier is purchased by the Navy for Cook's voyage and renamed Endeavour.

Captain Wallis returns from the Pacific to England with information about Tahiti.

The Endeavour *sails for Tahiti (30 July).*

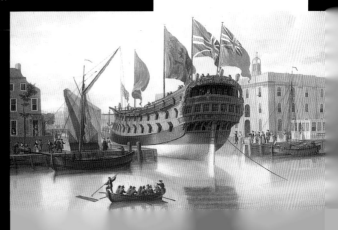

Endeavour

Cook's ship on his first voyage was sold in 1775 and broken up in 1793. For the last 30 years there have been attempts to build a replica, which was finally achieved at Fremantle in Australia between 1988 and 1994. She was built to the official plans in the National Maritime Museum and mainly by 18th-century methods, but using Australian timber and some modern techniques and artificial materials to enhance security of construction and rigging. Here she is shown over the Great Barrier Reef, which her predecessor struck in 1770, and on her voyage to Britain in 1997.

SAILING THE *ENDEAVOUR*

Men set the sails as they did 200 years ago. The rigging employs over 700 pulleys called blocks. Here a seaman frees a snag on the main sail.

THE FURNITURE AND EQUIPMENT

The Great Cabin (left) was shared by Cook with the naturalists and was where they did much of their botanical work. The officers' mess (right) has a folding table copied from one owned by Cook. Everything looks as it did.

Pictures courtesy of
HM Bark Endeavour Foundation, Fremantle
http://www.greenwich.uk.com/endeavour

CAPTAIN COOK
-A Time Line-

-1769-

The Transit of Venus is observed from Tahiti.

Endeavour *searches for the Great Southern Continent*

Cook discovers and starts charting New Zealand.

-1770-

Cook sails up the east coast of Australia.

-1771-

Endeavour *returns to England (12 June). Cook is chosen to command a second voyage.*

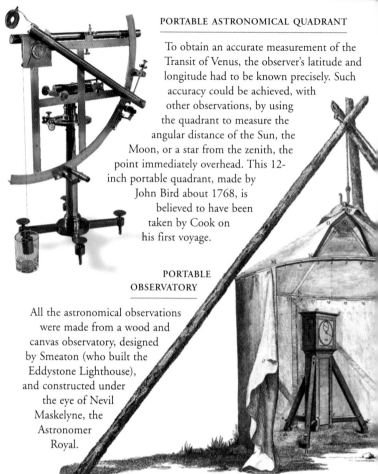

PORTABLE ASTRONOMICAL QUADRANT

To obtain an accurate measurement of the Transit of Venus, the observer's latitude and longitude had to be known precisely. Such accuracy could be achieved, with other observations, by using the quadrant to measure the angular distance of the Sun, the Moon, or a star from the zenith, the point immediately overhead. This 12-inch portable quadrant, made by John Bird about 1768, is believed to have been taken by Cook on his first voyage.

PORTABLE OBSERVATORY

All the astronomical observations were made from a wood and canvas observatory, designed by Smeaton (who built the Eddystone Lighthouse), and constructed under the eye of Nevil Maskelyne, the Astronomer Royal.

COOK'S CHART OF NEW ZEALAND

Cook charted North and South Islands so exactly that their shapes, as he represented them, are almost identical to those derived from modern mapping techniques. Almost all the place-names he proposed are still in use today.

QUEEN CHARLOTTE SOUND, NEW ZEALAND

After charting North Island, New Zealand, Cook put into this deep coastal inlet, swathed in forest, with abundant supplies of fresh water, fish, wild celery and scurvy grass. The local Maoris, 300-400 in number, were poorer than those in the north. They introduced themselves with a shower of stones and were obviously cannibals, but soon became friendly.

The Transit of Venus & New Zealand

The First Voyage, 1768-71

Cook and his companions set sail to observe the Transit of Venus in July 1768. They made for Tahiti, an island in the Pacific discovered by Captain Wallis, who had just returned from circumnavigating the globe before they set sail. The observations were successfully accomplished in June 1769, when Cook followed secret orders to look for the Great Southern Continent. Exploring south and west, the *Endeavour* discovered New Zealand, which Cook sailed all round. Repairs were effected in Queen Charlotte Sound where the Maoris were friendly and helpful. The charts Cook was to produce were not to be improved for another century.

ASTRONOMICAL CLOCK

In 1769 observers of the Transit of Venus in different parts of the world had to note the time the planet appeared to touch the disc of the Sun. Absolute accuracy of timing was essential. Thus, when observations were made a regulating clock was set up inside the portable observatory on shore. The clock was also used to check the running of marine chronometers. Its own accuracy had been checked by the Astronomer Royal at Greenwich before the voyage. The clock shown here went on at least one of Cook's voyages and is inscribed 'Royal Society No. 35 John Shelton, London'.

GREGORIAN REFLECTING TELESCOPE

To ensure accurate and comparable observations of the Transit of Venus, the Royal Society issued similar telescopes to all the observers it despatched to different parts of the world. This reflecting telescope was made in 1763 in London by James Short. Cook was equipped with two of them.

Australia
The First Voyage, 1768-71

Cook sailed west from New Zealand to explore Australia. Dutchmen had discovered the west coast, which they named New Holland, and the island of Tasmania over 150 years before. But the east coast was still unknown. Sighting its southern end, Cook sailed north, stopping to water in a bay so full of specimens for the naturalists that they called it Botany Bay. Further north, the *Endeavour* suddenly struck on part of the Great Barrier Reef. Getting off with difficulty, the ship had to be beached for six weeks for repairs.

Before sailing for home, Cook claimed the whole coast of New South Wales for King George III.

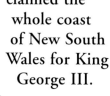

AUSTRALIAN FISH

Fish caught by the seamen and naturalists were both eaten and studied. The former enthusiastically helped the latter. The *Arripis Trutta*, shown here, grows to a metre long and was caught in the waters of Australia and New Zealand.

A KANGAROO

While repairing in the Endeavour River, they saw animals 'about the size of a greyhound, slender, mouse-coloured, swift, with a long tail, jumping like a hare'. They outpaced Banks's greyhound but several were shot and eaten. This one was painted by Sydney Parkinson.

THE *ENDEAVOUR* UNDER REPAIR

After the *Endeavour* got off the Great Barrier Reef, Cook found the 'Endeavour River' where the ship could be unloaded and beached for the repair of her hull.

AUSTRALIAN FLOWER

While the *Endeavour* was under repair, Joseph Banks gathered more specimens of plants and flowers, which were later presented to the British Museum. This one was called *Solanum viride*.

BOTANY BAY

Cook's first landing on Australian soil was in Botany Bay, where much of the vegetation, bird and animal life, was quite new. They met aborigines and caught large stingrays. Cook named the bay after the great quantity of botanical specimens collected by Joseph Banks and the botanist Daniel Solander.

QUARTERDECK OF A NAVAL VESSEL IN THE TROPICS

To shelter a ship's officers from the sun, canvas awnings were rigged over the quarterdeck. Common seamen were excluded from this deck unless performing some duty. Animals, taken to supply food, often became pets. This picture was painted about 1775 on a voyage from the West Indies to England but the quarterdeck of the *Endeavour* probably looked similar as she made her way up the east coast of Australia. Note the goat (for milk). Cook also took one – which had already sailed once round the world with Wallis!

The Great Southern Continent
The Second Voyage, 1772-75

Cook's first voyage had not disproved the existence of a Great Southern Continent and another expedition was soon equipped to solve this question. On 13 July 1772, this time with two ships, the *Resolution* and *Adventure*, Cook sailed for the Cape of Good Hope, then voyaged east through fog and ice, sleet and snow, at about latitude 60° South. Turning north, the two ships met at a rendezvous in Dusky Sound, New Zealand. Cook was able to find destinations precisely because he had been given the first accurate marine chronometer with which to find his longitude. The following Antarctic summer, 1773-74, Cook again sailed back into the ice and snow, reaching 71° South and finally proving that a habitabl southern continent really did not exist.

PICKERSGILL HARBOUR, DUSKY SOUND, NEW ZEALAND

Returning from Antarctic waters in March 1773, Cook moored the *Resolution* in a small creek 'so near the shore as to reach it by a large tree which growed in a horizontal direction over the water so long that the top of it reached our gunwale'.

The creek had plentiful supplies of fresh water and fish, to the delight of the seamen. One can be seen here returning from the astronomical observation tent that was set up on shore.

PICKING UP ICE

Voyaging through Antarctic waters, Cook's crews replenished their water supply by cutting ice from icebergs, which they called 'ice islands'. In the absence of land in these latitudes, they also shot sea birds to obtain fresh meat. Hodges drew the scene in January 1773.

COOK'S CHRONOMETER

At his fourth attempt, John Harrison succeeded in making a practical and reliable marine chronometer. It was tested on a sea voyage in 1761 and over four weeks was out by only five seconds. However, Harrison was awarded only half the Board of Longitude's £20,000 prize; for the chronometer also had to be capable of precise reproduction. In 1772 Cook therefore took with him this copy by Larcum Kendall, on trial. Its accuracy permitted Harrison to get the other half of his prize in 1773.

THE CAPE OF GOOD HOPE

Cook was accompanied on this voyage by the 28-year old artist, William Hodges, who painted this view from the deck of the *Resolution* on their voyage south. The *Adventure* can be seen inshore, with her sails aback and Cape Town behind. Hodges was to paint many more dramatic landscapes on the voyage.

MAORI CLUB AXE

Although generally friendly, the Maori peoples of New Zealand could be dangerous. In December 1773 Captain Furneaux in the *Adventure* missed a rendezvous with Cook's *Resolution*, so that his ship was alone in Queen Charlotte Sound, New Zealand. The ship's cutter and ten men were sent to get provisions but they were all killed and some were eaten. In their attack the Maoris probably used a club axe of the type shown.

TAHITIAN FLAPS

This long-haired fly swat - 'very ingeniously wrought' - was obtained by trade by Joseph Banks from an island close to Tahiti; the flanking figures are handles.

The Pacific Peoples...
The Second Voyage, 1772-75

During the Antarctic winters, Cook explored and charted many of the islands of the Pacific. Both in 1773 and 1774 he was welcomed back to Tahiti, where a favourite anchorage was Matavai Bay. In 1773 the crews of both *Resolution* and *Adventure* were sickly with scurvy and Cook spread a sail as an awning on the beach, where the sick could recover in comfort. The hills inland gave the artist of the voyage, William Hodges, a trained landscape painter, subject matter to his taste. The splendour of the scenes he painted did much to make Europeans think the Pacific islands were paradise. The Tahitians were depicted in noble, classical poses, but Cook suffered much from their eagerness to acquire items from the ships, by theft if not trade. The women pursued this practice as much as the men, and with much success owing to their willingness to pay for shirts and nails with sexual favours.

Resolution and *Adventure* in Matavai Bay, Tahiti, in 1773; by William Hodges.

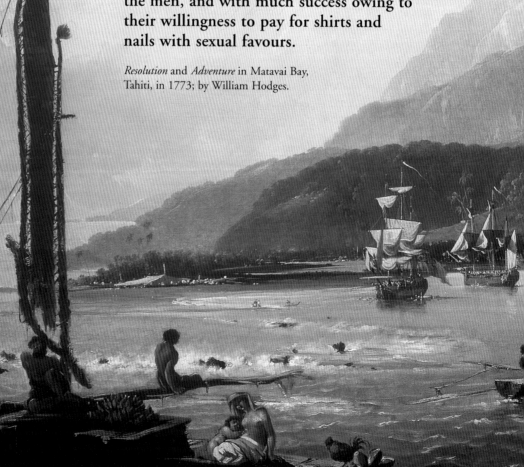

OMAI

Omai was from Huahine, near Tahiti. Intelligent and friendly, he acted as an interpreter and wished to visit Britain. Captain Furneaux in the *Adventure* brought him back to London where he became a celebrity before being returned to Tahiti in 1777.

BAKING BREADFRUIT

The breadfruit tree grows naturally in Tahiti. The Tahitians eat the fruit and are here shown cooking it. Joseph Banks proposed growing the fruit in the West Indies to feed plantation slaves. William Bligh, who accompanied Cook on his second voyage, delivered the trees in 1791 but the slaves shunned the fruit because of its bland taste.

At Tahiti in 1774 Cook came across the assembled fleet of war canoes and galleys - over 300 vessels - drawn up for inspection by the principal chief. They carried flags and streamers, and 'made a grand and noble appearance such as was never seen before in this sea'. Cook watched as, lashed together in divisions, they practised paddling furiously to land together on the beach where they engaged in mock battle. After William Hodges had drawn them, Cook had the pleasure of going on board several.

CAPTAIN COOK
-A Time Line-

-1772-73-

Resolution *and* Adventure *search for the Great Southern Continent.*

-1773-

Resolution *circles the South Pacific, discovering the Tonga Islands.*

-1773-74-

Cook reaches latitude 71° South, looking for the Great Southern Continent.

-1774-

A wider Pacific circle discovers Easter Island, the Marquesas and New Hebrides.

-1775-

Cook returns to England (30 July).

FOUR
TONGAN
WAR CLUBS

Although the Tongan people were friendly to Cook, their chieftains had to defend their islands. Because they travelled and fought from canoes, paddles sometimes served as war clubs. These clubs are thought to have been collected by Cook, probably by trade, for the Tongan people had an insatiable appetite for nails. Cook's voyages were the first to bring back collections of such ethnographic items, giving rise to comparisons and the study of anthropology.

THE LANDING AT EROMANGA, NEW HEBRIDES

In August 1774 Cook landed to ask for wood and water but was met by a great group armed with clubs, darts, stones, bows and arrows. He suspected the worst and stepped back into his boat, upon which the crowd surged forward, shooting and throwing missiles, and tried to drag the boat up the beach. Cook's musket misfired and he had to order others to fire. Four men fell, but Cook's boat escaped.

...The Pacific Peoples
The Second Voyage, 1772-75

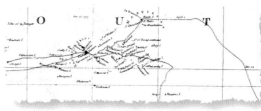

Exploring west of Tahiti in 1773, Cook discovered the Tonga group, where the people were so friendly he called them the Friendly Islands.

Further east in 1774 he found Easter Island with its giant statues, and the Marquesas, islands known to the Spaniards but whose location had never been charted. Returning west again, he found the New Hebrides, inhabited by Melanesians and less friendly than the Polynesians so far encountered. These island groups had a special beauty, with many unusual flowering trees and shrubs, including at Tahiti the breadfruit tree. However, drinking water was often scarce, while underwater coral reefs made navigation perilous. Cook's achievement was thus the greater and he was to be much honoured on his return home.

THE MONUMENTS OF EASTER ISLAND

In March 1774 Cook sent 27 men to explore the island. They found seven stone figures, four of which were still standing, with three overturned, perhaps by earthquake. The figures represented men to their waist, with large ears. They were about 18 feet high and 5 feet wide, 'ill-shaped' and, had large 'hats' of red rock on their heads, like some Egyptian gods. One hat measured over five feet in diameter. The figures appeared to mark burying places, for among the stones were several human bones, as shown in Hodges' painting.

The Pacific Further Explored
The Third Voyage, 1776-80

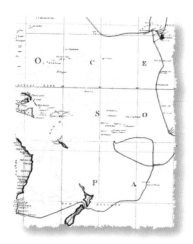

In July 1776, a year after returning home, Cook sailed again for the Pacific. This was partly to return Omai to Tahiti, partly because there was hope of finding a North-West Passage from the Pacific to the Atlantic for trading purposes, and partly to examine some desolate islands discovered by the French, Britain's enemy, near the Cape of Good Hope. The *Resolution* and *Discovery*, his two ships, made for Tasmania (then known as Van Diemen's Land) and New Zealand, before sailing through the Tonga Islands to Tahiti. Aiming for the west coast of Canada, Cook pressed north at the end of the year, spending Christmas 1777 on a coral atoll, Christmas Island, before discovering the Sandwich Islands, including Hawaii.

STONE TOOLS AND TATTOOING INSTRUMENTS, TAHITI

The tools and instruments in use in the Pacific Islands were Stone-Age in their sophistication. European society, which took the Bible literally, assumed that primitive societies were closer to nature and to the innocence of the Garden of Eden. However, the islanders' practice of human sacrifice, their sexual freedoms and thefts from Cook's ships, conflicted with Christian ideals and made Europeans question their own literal beliefs.

KENDALL'S THIRD MARINE CHRONOMETER

Cook continued to benefit from the rapid improvement of navigational equipment. In the *Discovery* he took another chronometer made by Larcum Kendall, who had been requested by the Board of Longitude to attempt to improve upon his previous copies of John Harrison's prize-winning model. The new 'watch machine' was simpler and mass production would permit merchant shipping and traders to follow where Cook had been.

A HUMAN SACRIFICE AT TAHITI

At this, his fourth visit to Tahiti, Cook was honoured by being taken to a human sacrifice intended to assist the chief in a local war. He made careful observations. No women were present and Cook had to remove his hat. Drums were beaten and prayers were uttered. A man, bruised from being beaten to death, was trussed to a pole. One of his eyes was ceremoniously eaten, before he was buried; then a dog was sacrificed and presented to their *atua* or god.

A NIGHT DANCE BY WOMEN IN THE TONGA OR FRIENDLY ISLES

Making his third visit to the Friendly Isles, Cook was entertained as an honoured guest. The Tongan men sat in a semi-circle and began a song with a rhythm beaten with hollow pieces of bamboo. Then younger women came and encircled the men, singing and dancing, their bodies shining in the torchlight: 'the most beautiful forms that imagination can conceive'. Quickening songs interspersed with savage shouts, even a little female 'indecency', made it an exhilarating performance.

CAPTAIN COOK
- A Time Line -

~1776~

Cook begins his third Pacific voyage and sails south in the Resolution, *in company with the* Discovery *(12 July).*

Britain's American colonies declare their independence.

~1777~

Cook returns to New Zealand, Tonga and Tahiti, and discovers Christmas Island.

~1778~

After discovering Hawaii, Cook explores the north-west coast of North America, and passes through the Bering Strait.

THE NOOTKA SOUND PEOPLE

Large numbers of natives visited the ships daily, some clearly having come from a long distance away. On first appearance they generally went through the same ceremony. They first paddled with all their strength around the ships; a chief, his face covered with a mask of either a human or an animal face, then stood up with a spear or rattle in his hand and shouted a greeting. Sometimes this was followed by a song in which they all joined and made 'very agreeable harmony', upon which they came closer and began to trade.

POLAR BEAR

Cook's companions spotted a white bear in the arctic. John Webber, the artist, was only 24 when they set out, but he was accomplished at rapidly drawing broad landscapes and natural objects with precise detail. Here he caught the huge size and dangerous character of the animal.

REFITTING THE SHIPS

The *Resolution*'s fore and mizzen masts had to be replaced, and the rigging of her mainmast had to be renewed. Sheer-legs were thus set up on the *Resolution*'s deck to get out the defective masts. New masts were cut and fashioned on shore, where smiths forged new fittings on the beach.

A SEA OTTER

The sea otter's lustrous skins were much prized. Russian traders had been busy buying the pelts from eskimos and indians since 1741, when Bering discovered the strait that bears his name. The Chinese paid high prices for them. Cook's report of the trade prompted British merchants in China, then other Europeans and Americans, to mount trading ventures. Soon the north Pacific was alive with ships.

North~West Canada & Alaska

The Third Voyage, 1776-80

Off the Canadian coast early in 1778, Cook first found a safe bay, later called Nootka Sound, (below left) in which to refit the *Resolution* and *Discovery*. He then coasted north, entering every inlet in search of a North-West Passage. Everywhere he landed, Cook met the Indian people who lived on these coasts. Rounding Alaska, he pressed through the Bering Strait dividing the continents of Asia and America and, peering through persistent fogs, entered the Arctic Sea. At 20° North he met the pack-ice and, unwilling to let his ships get trapped, turned back. Planning to return the next summer, he then sailed for the Sandwich Islands, where Hawaii seemed to offer a welcoming winter resting place.

SURVEY WORK

As soon as the ships were moored, the portable observatories were set up on an elevated rock for the astromoners to take their observations. The longitude of the cove was settled with the utmost care, for this position would become a bearing for further navigation. In front of the tents, surveying work began, to chart and map the waters and terrain of the sound.

BEAVER BOWL, INLAID WITH SHELL

The indians brought fish, furs, weapons, bladders full of oil, and even human skulls to exchange for any sort of metal - knives, chisels, nails, buttons. They stole as well as traded, and even Cook's own gold watch was taken, though later recovered. The greatest desire of the seamen was for sea-otter pelts. This wooden bowl, carved in the shape of a beaver, was probably obtained in Nootka Sound.

SHOOTING 'SEA-HORSES'

Penetrating through the Bering Strait in August 1778, in latitude 20° North, Cook met an ice field, inhabited by 'sea-horses' or walruses. To obtain fresh meat, boats were sent from both ships to kill twelve of the great beasts. Cook was delighted and, to ensure the meat was eaten, stopped all normal rations except bread.

The Death of Cook

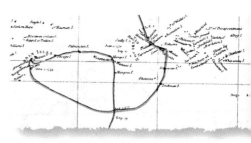

*A*t Hawaii Cook was greeted like a god. The Hawaiians were expecting their god, Lono, to arrive on a floating island with trees, not unlike the *Resolution*. Gifts and trade abounded but so also did thefts. Cook tried to punish the culprits and retrieve stolen equipment, sometimes by taking hostages. By February 1779 awe for Cook, and his own patience, had both grown thin. While trying to retrieve a stolen ship's cutter, Cook was suddenly killed. Captain Clerke of the *Discovery* finished looking for the North-West Passage but was unsuccessful. Cook's voyages had nevertheless opened the largest ocean in the world to European trade and settlement. They had contributed to knowledge of different peoples and cultures, of the Earth, its plants and animals, and of its place in the universe. Moreover, they had been achieved with little loss of seamen's lives and respect for other races. Cook set new standards for all explorers to follow.

HAWAIIAN SPEAR

The Hawaiians, like other Pacific islanders, originally had only wood and stone weapons, against which they defended themselves with woven mats. These were no match for European firearms and swords made of metal. However, realising the usefulness of metal they traded and stole it whenever possible, and made metal daggers. Cook was stabbed with one in the struggle before his death. Otherwise, the crowd by which he was overwhelmed was armed with spears and stones.

THE DEATH OF COOK

When the *Discovery*'s cutter was taken on 14 February 1779, Cook went ashore to take the local chief hostage for its return. A hostile crowd gathered, which grew angrier when Cook himself fired at a man who threatened him, upon which the Hawaiians launched themselves on Cook's party. Cook was hit from behind with a club, then stabbed and drowned.

COOK'S SUCCESSOR IN THE PACIFIC

In 1789, William Bligh, sailing master of the *Resolution* on the second voyage suffered a mutiny after returning to Tahiti in the *Bounty* to collect breadfruit for the West Indies.

COOK UNDERMINED

Cook normally treated the Pacific islanders with reasoned patience. At Hawaii, however, he started to act out of character and decided on a sudden descent on the Hawaiian village. He took armed marines and ordered their firearms to be loaded and fired to kill. It is now thought that strain and the poor diet of three long voyages, and possibly illness, had undermined his understanding and caution.

~1779~
Cook returns to Hawaii and is killed.

~1780~
After exploring the north-west coast of the Pacific, and again penetrating the Bering Strait in search of a North-West Passage, his ships return to England (4 Oct).

~1783~
The American War of Independence ends.

~1787-89~
Bligh's return to Tahiti in the Bounty *to collect breadfruit ends in mutiny off Tofoa.*

BRITISH PISTOL

This pistol is the sort issued to sea officers and Cook would have carried one as necessary. When he was killed, he was carrying a two-barrelled musket, one barrel loaded with 'small shot', the other with ball. He was accompanied by a lieutenant and nine marines, all armed with muskets. The number of guns was intended to threaten. The disadvantage of these weapons in a crowd situation was that they could not be reloaded quickly.

POEDUA - A HOSTAGE

In November 1777, two seamen deserted in the Society Islands and, to force the islanders to return them, Cook took hostage the 15-year-old daughter of the local chief, her brother and her husband. Among friends, the three captives were not alarmed, but their father quickly secured the deserters. John Webber painted the girl's portrait.

DID YOU KNOW?

Why scurvy was a problem for so long
We now know that scurvy is caused by a deficiency of Vitamin C, usually from lack of fresh fruit and vegetables. However, vitamins were not identified until 1915. Before this fresh meat was also known to prevent the disease, often because animals had eaten green fodder before slaughter. Citrus fruit juice (ascorbic acid) was adopted against scurvy by the Admiralty in 1795 but before that fresh air, dry clothing, warmth and exercise were also thought to help prevent it. There was thus much confusion about its exact cause.

How time gives longitude Each day (24 hours) the Earth turns through 360°, from west to east; that is, it turns through 15° of longitude every hour and 1° every 4 minutes. A place that has a 4-minute difference in time at noon from a starting point (or 'prime meridian') to east or west - noon in each spot being when the Sun is exactly overhead - is 1° of longitude away. Thus, accurate east/west time variations between places can be converted into relative distances and positions of longitude.

Where the design of ships like the *Endeavour* **came from** The 'cat-built' ships constructed for the coal trade on the north-east coast of England in Cook's day, were based on types captured from the Dutch in the Anglo-Dutch wars of 1652-74. Because of their shallow waters and the need to load and unload vessels sitting on the foreshore, and because the Dutch grew rich from carrying bulky cargoes round the world, they designed very strong, flat-bottomed, roomy ships which proved ideal as a pattern for later English colliers.

Where Cook is buried The Hawaiians partly ate then burnt Cook's body, according to custom. A few days later, when relations with his men had improved, they returned most of his bones. On 21 February 1779, his remains were buried at sea in a full naval ceremony, just off-shore from Kileakekua Bay where he was killed. A monument there marks the site of his death.

What happened to Cook's wife Elizabeth Cook was 38 when her husband died. She survived him by 56 years and died, aged 93, on 13 May 1835, 72 years after their marriage in Barking church. She remained deeply proud of 'Mr Cook', as she always spoke of him. Sadly, all their six children had died by 1794.

ACKNOWLEDGEMENTS

Consultant Editor: Pieter van der Merwe, National Maritime Museum.
We would like to thank: Graham Rich, Tracey Pennington and Deon Fullard for their assistance.
Copyright © 1997 ticktock Publishing Ltd. Text copyright © 1997 National Maritime Museum.
First published in Great Britain by ticktock Publishing Ltd., Great Britain. All rights reserved.
No part of this publication may be reproduced, stored in a retrieval system, or transmitted in any form or by any means, electronic, mechanical, photocopying, recording or otherwise, without prior written permission of the copyright owner.
Printed in Hong Kong.

For further information on the subjects/pictures in this booklet contact: National Maritime Museum, Greenwich, London SE10 9NF. Tel: (0)20 8858 4422. Fax: (0)20 8312 6632. http://www.nmm.ac.uk

Picture Credits: t=top, b=bottom, c=centre, l=left, r=right, OBC=outside back cover
We are grateful to the National Maritime Museum, London for permission to reproduce their copyright photographs for *Captain Cook & His Exploration of the Pacific*, with the exception of the following: Cary Wolinsky (The Natural History Museum, London); 10cb. Richard Polden; 14ct. John Lancaster; 14l. Antonia Macarthur; 14cb. David Doubilet (National Geographic Society); 14/15. Robert Garvey; 14/15b, OBCcr. Joe Tyrrell; 15br. The Natural History Museum, London; 18c & OBC, 19c & OBC. Cary Wolinsky (National Geographic Society); 19t, 23tl. By courtesy of the National Portrait Gallery, London; 30cb. By permission of the British Library (K51994); OBCcb.

Every effort has been made to trace the copyright holders and we apologise in advance for any unintentional omissions. We would be pleased to insert the appropriate acknowledgement in any subsequent edition of this publication.

A CIP catalogue record for this book is available from the British Library. ISBN 1 86007 032 9 (pbk) 1 86007 325 5 (hbk).

snapping-turtle
guide

INDEX